Happy Birthday Jo
Enjoy !
Lots of
your xo.

Just Turn Up

Georgina Smith

Trafford
PUBLISHING

Order this book online at www.trafford.com/07-2590
or email orders@trafford.com

Most Trafford titles are also available at major online book retailers.

© Copyright 2007 Georgina Smith.
All rights reserved. No part of this publication may be reproduced, stored in a retrieval
system, or transmitted, in any form or by any means, electronic, mechanical, photocopying,
recording, or otherwise, without the written prior permission of the author.

Note for Librarians: A cataloguing record for this book is available from Library
and Archives Canada at www.collectionscanada.ca/amicus/index-e.html

Printed in Victoria, BC, Canada

ISBN: 978-1-4251-5755-5

*We at Trafford believe that it is the responsibility of us all, as both individuals
and corporations, to make choices that are environmentally and socially sound.
You, in turn, are supporting this responsible conduct each time you purchase a
Trafford book, or make use of our publishing services. To find out how you are
helping, please visit www.trafford.com/responsiblepublishing.html*

*Our mission is to efficiently provide the world's finest, most comprehensive
book publishing service, enabling every author to experience success.
To find out how to publish your book, your way, and have it available
worldwide, visit us online at www.trafford.com/10510*

Trafford
PUBLISHING™

www.trafford.com

North America & international
toll-free: 1 888 232 4444 (USA & Canada)
phone: 250 383 6864 ♦ fax: 250 383 6804
email: info@trafford.com

The United Kingdom & Europe
phone: +44 (0)1865 722 113 ♦ local rate: 0845 230 9601
facsimile: +44 (0)1865 722 868 ♦ email: info.uk@trafford.com

10 9 8 7 6 5 4 3 2

Dedication

To Mike

with love

❧ Introduction ❧

Thank you for choosing my book about meditation. If you have thought about
trying to meditate, or you have tried and given up because it doesn't seem to
work, then this is the CD and book for you. I'll let you into a secret. Anyone can
learn to meditate. It really is simple.
You only need to read the first chapter once, and then switch on the CD and
away you go. It's as easy as that!
My CD and book show you the way to gradually clear your mind of stress and
negativity, past, present and future. I am not promising you a quick
transformation, as I don't think it is possible to clear years of negative thoughts in
a few days. However you will soon start to notice that you feel more positive,
more at ease within, and more accepting of yourself and others. More often, you
will find that other people around you will comment on a positive change in you.

The CD takes you straight to the meditation technique and the book is here to
provide the answers to any queries that may arise.

I am giving you a skill for life. Once you have learned my technique it will always
be there for you.

I offer you the benefit of my twenty years experience of meditation, and wish that
I had been given such simple guidance as this when I first started.

There is only one difficult thing about meditation and that is getting round to
doing it!

So just turn up!

How to make best use of this CD and book

Before using the CD for the first time, I suggest you read the first part of the book, 'Getting Started'. This gives you practical advice on preparing to meditate.
There are no introductions or explanations on the CD. I have done this deliberately as the meditation tracks are sufficient unto themselves in their simplicity and I personally have found it irritating to hear preliminary instructions over and over. It is more helpful to switch on the track you require and just meditate, instead of going into all the whys and wherefores.
The CD has six tracks of meditations. Tracks 1 and 2 are for use everyday, the remainder are for occasional use as suggested in the book.
On each track you will hear me speaking intermittently to help you meditate, and there are periods of silence. Meditation is

done in silence in order to be alert to
what is happening within. When you hear the
sound of a bell you will know that I
am going to bring the meditation session to a
close.
I suggest you start with the ten minute meditation (track 1) for a week or so
before increasing to the twenty minute (track
2). I do not know why it should be,
but a meditation for twenty minutes seems to
be the natural length of time per
session.
As your meditation practice becomes established you will find what time is best
for you, and this may vary depending on your
frame of mind and daily activities
and commitments. It doesn't matter, trust the
process and meditate regularly to
get the best results.
You will find as you become more comfortable
with the process that you will be able to use
the technique anywhere anytime to take yourself to the stillness within.
Once you have settled into a routine of regular
meditation, start to meditate
without using the CD. It is not my intention for
you to depend on my voice for

your meditation practice. I am here to get you started, and the book is here to answer questions that may arise during meditation. I suggest you dip in and out of it as a reference rather than reading it from beginning to end.

❧ Contents ☙

Part One - Getting Started

Part Two - About Meditation

Part Three - Hindrances to meditation

Part Four- Other meditation techniques

❧ Part One ❧

Getting Started

1.1 Where to meditate?

You will be able to meditate in any quiet place, indoors or outdoors.

Until your meditation practise is fully established, I would recommend you meditate in the same place each time.

Choose a place in your home where you can feel comfortable and quiet, somewhere you can easily go to everyday and identify as your special place for meditation. Make your meditation area pleasing for you, so you know you are going to feel happy to spend some time there. In my meditation spot, I like to light a candle and have a small vase of flowers on the table. This gives me the right triggers to start meditating.

Sit on an upright chair, such as a dining chair. If you wish, you can sit cross-legged on a cushion on the floor or on the bed. As long as you are comfortable, and as long as your head is not supported by a cushion that's fine.

It is not good to lie down or slump in an easy chair to meditate as you quickly go into sleep mode!

Have your CD player to hand with the controls in easy reach. Place a little clock on a table or shelf nearby.

Check that the phone is on answer phone, switch off your mobile, and let pets and family know that you want to be quiet for about twenty minutes.

1.2 When to meditate

Plan to go to your meditation place once a day at about the same time of day.

Then the meditation time becomes part of your daily routine.

When you prepare to meditate, be sure you are comfortable. Be neither too warm nor too cold, neither too hungry nor too full. The meditation technique is not for relaxation so I find it is better not to meditate after having alcohol as it causes sleepiness.

I suggest you avoid meditating just before you go to bed, as this can bring on sleepiness, too .

Some people prefer to meditate in the early morning, others in the early evening.

Try both times to see which suits you best. When you realise the benefits of meditation you will want to practise twice a day, and this is very beneficial.

To start with, begin by meditating for ten

minutes and gradually increase to twenty minutes each session.

1.3 Preparing to meditate

It isn't necessary to wear any special clothing, such as a track suit or yoga clothes, just be comfortable. Because you are going to be sitting still, you may feel cold after a while, so have a wrap or a cardigan to hand. You may wish to remove your shoes or change into slippers, and you may prefer to take off your glasses.

Preparing yourself for meditation is always part of the session. Each track on the CD starts with preparation for meditation. You will hear me saying:-

You are sitting on an upright chair, in your quiet space. Make yourself comfortable, checking that both feet are firmly on the ground. Place your hands on top of your legs, or if it feels right for you, link your hands in your lap.

Spend a few moments thinking how enjoyable it is to be in your meditation place.

Praise yourself for turning up! Accept the fact that this meditation is really going to benefit you.

Gently close your eyes. You may notice that your eyes are moving, even when your eyelids are closed. So imagine your gaze is resting on the bridge of your nose.

Smile to yourself. You might think this is a bit silly, but try it and you will see that it brings a feeling of ease.'

It is important to prepare for meditation in this way, as it helps to settle the mind for the work ahead.

1.4 After meditation

Each track on the CD ends with bringing your awareness back into your body.

Always include five minutes rest after you have finished meditating.

Your body and mind have been quiet so they need time to adjust before you start any activity.

In the morning, deep breathing and gentle physical stretching are a helpful way to start the day after you have meditated.

If you do a meditation in the early evening, you may feel sleepy afterwards. I know I sometimes do, so I just have a nap in the chair for a few minutes or lie down on the floor with a cushion under my head.

Afterwards you will feel very refreshed and you will be ready to enjoy the rest of your evening.

❧ Part Two ❦

About Meditation

2.1 What is meditation?

Meditation is going to stillness within in full awareness. Here one experiences peace and can see the mind for what it is -a wonderful tool of creation.

I have been regularly practising meditation for over twenty years, and teaching meditation techniques for five years. Over the years I have tried a variety of techniques, and chosen those which suit me, and have come up with my own versions. The methods I teach are tried and tested, and have served me well.

They are very suitable for busy people with hectic lifestyles as most of us have.

I think my versions should suit almost anyone regardless of culture, religious beliefs or background.

My 'bread and butter' meditation is observing my breathing. I call it this because it is the first and last part of every other technique, and it is the one I use every day.

This simple action of observing my breathing takes me to inner quietness. My body and mind quieten down to stillness and there I am in the infinite stillness.

There is no thought, no sensations, no action, just being. *Simple awareness.*

Then thoughts, feelings arise again. I notice them, and perhaps get involved in them. When I realise this, I start over again, witnessing my breathing — going to stillness. I call stillness my default setting. My thoughts and feelings change all the time. I am this and then that, but stillness is always there, always the same.

I use and teach other meditation techniques, too, for different purposes. But I always use my 'bread and butter' breathing meditation everyday. My advice to the beginner is to do this too. It is too easy to get sidetracked trying out all the various techniques. The mind charms you this way. So take control of the mind rather than allowing the mind to control you!

Further on in the book, I explain other techniques for you to use for specific times, and some of these are also on the CD.

Let us get back to basics. Every meditation

session is a different experience and you will soon realise this. You may experience fidgeting or mental busyness at one session and the next session may be peaceful and comfortable.

So have no expectation, because each session is different. Trust that the meditation is doing the business of clearing stress, worry and negativity. The process is very gentle so you need to accept that meditation is no quick fix.

Thoughts and sensations in meditation are normal; they are part of the natural cycle of meditation practise.

There is no need for concentration and effort, and this is a very common misconception about meditation.

When people question me about meditation, I often find there is misunderstanding about the nature of it.

Again I can only give my own view of the definition. Meditation is moving to a state of quiet alert awareness where the mind is still but one is witnessing. It is not self hypnosis, nor a state of auto suggestion, nor a trance.

It is not contemplation, which I interpret as quietly dwelling on an idea or an object to gain understanding.

It is not creative visualisation, where one takes an imaginary journey to a pleasant scenario in order to explore aspects of the psyche.

Nor is it for relaxation through music or storytelling. These techniques have great value in themselves but should not be mistaken for meditation.

2.2 Why Meditate?

Since the second World War, the emphasis of the media in the western world has been to drive us to the pursuit of happiness. If you eat this food, drink this wine, take these pills you will be happy. If you buy this car or take that holiday you will be happy. Isn't it easy to be drawn into this way of thinking! This happiness relies on expectation and is short lived. How often I used to return from a holiday feeling happy, and within a couple of days back at work I was back to not being happy, feeling that I had never been away.

This happiness thing is so elusive! The word 'happiness' has so many connotations around it. What I have concluded is that I don't want to be happy all the time. Instead I wish to be at ease within myself. What is it that causes unease within myself? Past negative experiences that created guilt, anger, resentment; present negative judgements, future negative thoughts of fear, worry and what ifs.

During meditation we become aware of our thoughts and feelings, and the meditation process works by releasing negativity in a very gentle way, bringing one to a state of ease within oneself. This has to be the best reason for meditating! When we are at ease within, everyone we come into contact with benefits too.

2.3 What does meditation do?

Scientific studies have been carried out to show that brain activity changes during meditation, and there is evidence that blood pressure and heart rate drop to a resting state. Meditation is frequently recommended for patients having cardiac rehabilitation.

Some teachers state that stress is stored in the nervous system of the body, and that stress is released during meditation. I think there is some truth in this. From my own experience, I feel that I have been able to let go of long held, past negativity during meditation.

For the sceptic, one could provide scientific proof of changes in mind and body during meditation. For those holding religious beliefs, meditation practises of different types are a form of devotion.

For those who regularly practise meditation, there are some effects common to all. One feels more relaxed about life in general, more positive, more vital. Some people with sleep problems find meditation helps. Certain anxiety states are improved.

For me, meditation has changed my inner life for the better. I had lived for years with what I can only describe as inner aloneness, darkness and self dislike, that I kept at bay by being busy, busy, busy. Once I stopped being busy the emptiness welled up again.

After I had been meditating regularly for a few months, I experienced a knowing and the feelings of emptiness, self dislike left me, never to return. I no longer felt the need to be needed, or that I needed this or that to be happy.

I have since read that other people who meditate have similar experiences.

It is not easy to describe what I mean by a 'knowing'. It wasn't a bolt of lightning experience, rather a flower slowly unfurling. Now don't misunderstand me. I still experience the ups and downs of being a human being involved in family life and the world around me. I still have desires, likes and dislikes, but now my base line is ease and harmony. I have compassion for the past and no fear of the future.

This is what regular meditation has done for me, and I would love you to have the same.

2.4 Placing an intention into meditation

Systems of positive thinking and affirmations have been in vogue for quite a few years. There are many management techniques and personal development programs, each having a different slant on being positive. I am all for any system that encourages people to think positively but I am not totally sure of the effectiveness of the techniques. From my own experience, it is very easy to change one's thought patterns and behaviour for a short time with the encouragement and guidance of a teacher, and a period of training, but as soon as the impetus has gone, one quickly reverts to old patterns of thought and habit.

Most of us want a quick, easy and painless way out of our problems with the least effort on our part, or better still for someone else to sort it for us!

So it is very attractive to buy into a system that promises instant transformation.

On rare occasions, an individual experiences a sudden dramatic change in their thinking, but when you hear their story, s/he has been to the depths of despair due to depression, drugs or alcohol. Having experienced this transformation, the person carries a fervour to help others to change. I am not one of these exceptional people. Most of us are living ordinary lives and trying to improve our lot little by little.

Having read my views on positive thinking courses, you may wonder why I am now suggesting you use a positive thought (or affirmation) during your meditation. The reason is that it seems to be more effective. My explanation is this; when you whisper a clear message in a quiet space it is more likely to be heard than at a noisy party.

If you really wish to bring something to yourself or change something about your self, then this technique is very useful and easy.

So how do you go about it? First of all, decide precisely what it is you wish to happen. Then write it down in one sentence. If there is any word that has a negative connotation in the sentence re-write it so that it is positive.

Secondly, the intention must be for you and no-one else. You cannot organize someone else's life pattern however much you would like to!

Here are some examples of negative and positive intentions

Negative - "I intend to lose weight"

Positive - "I choose to be slim"

Negative - "I intend to stop worrying about my health"

Positive - "I intend to enjoy being alive"

Negative - "I wish my partner would be more considerate to me"

Positive - "I intend to see the good qualities in my partner"

When you are satisfied with the sentence you have written down, start your meditation. When you reach a moment of quietness, then recite your sentence of intention (either out loud or in you mind, it doesn't matter). Do not dwell on it, just let it go. Continue with your meditation as usual. The effects of the intention may not be noticeable at first, but over time you will become aware that your intention is working for you.

Use track 3 on the CD for this meditation technique.

2.5 Questions and requests

You can also use questions and requests in a similar way to placing an intention.

I have done this many times with great results, particularly when facing difficult problems.

Once again, write down your question or request in a positive way and in the stillness of your meditation, say your sentence and let it go; then continue with your meditation.

Here are a few examples:

Negative – What can I do to get rid of my back pain?

Positive – What can I do to make my back supple and strong?

Negative – How can I resolve my difficulties with my boss?

Positive – How can I improve my working relationship with my boss?

Negative – How can I get out of debt?

Positive – How can I improve my finances?

The answer to your question may not be immediate, but you will be amazed how quickly replies turn up. It may be a new idea just pops into your head, or you see or hear something that gives you a new slant on your problem, or the problem just disappears.

When you desire something in particular, use a request in your meditation. It is important to be clear and positive, otherwise things you have requested will turn up not quite how you want them, but that is because you have not made a clear request.

If you ask to go on a luxury cruise, you may find you are offered a ferry trip to Calais and back. 'That's not luxury' you say, but it is compared with a rowing boat!

You may wish to ask for a new job opportunity. It is important to define exactly want you mean otherwise all types of job offers will come your way, many not being what you really want!

Some of my students have asked for a new meaningful relationship, which has happened but not worked out. When I have questioned them about what they really want, it is obvious that they are unsure or unclear. This is the message that they have sent out, hence their difficulties.

So you can request good things in general, such as, "May all good things in life come my way" or you can be specific "please help me to buy a new silver soft-topped two-seater sports car".

Whatever your request, be clear and sincerely mean it. Then see what opportunities come your way.

Use track 4 on the CD for this meditation technique

❧ Part Three ❧

Hindrances to meditation

3.1 The busy mind

The commonest problem people complain of is too many thoughts in meditation.

Thoughts are normal in meditation. We are thinking almost all the time and for the most part we are unaware of what we are thinking or that we are thinking. So when we come to sit and meditate, we become aware of the mental activity that has been going on all day. It is said that a large proportion of our thoughts are repetitions of previous thoughts, and we are not consciously aware of this. Sitting down to meditate with the idea of being quiet brings our thoughts to a conscious level.

If you have had a very busy day with a lot of mental stimulation take longer in preparation. Try a few stretching exercises, or listen to gentle music, or read an inspiring text. Allow your body to settle a few minutes, and then the mind will calm down.

3.2 Inability to concentrate or focus

Another common complaint from beginners is 'I just can't concentrate or focus'.

This is a misunderstanding, because concentration and focus imply effort. It takes effort to turn up in your meditation chair every day, but once you have done your preparation, the meditation requires no effort, no concentration. You are just noticing, watching for the out breath. This is the key that opens the door to stillness. Thoughts arise and the mind starts judging or planning or whatever.

This is normal, so when you notice this, take the mind gently, like a naughty toddler, back to watching for the out breath. Gently without scolding take the mind away from its preoccupations back to noticing the out breath.

No forcing, no concentration. Be gentle with yourself and enjoy.

3.3 Putting off meditation

Do you know, there are some things I will put off doing until I really have to, such as mending clothes, filling in forms, filing my nails. I notice myself thinking 'I'll just tidy up, mop the floor, prepare the vegetables etc, and then I'll do the mending'.

Of course, I manage to run out of time or put it off for another day. The amount of mental energy I use thinking about how I really should do the hated job is amazing, and I beat myself up about it. When the job is done I'm astonished at how quickly it was done and how good I feel when it is completed.

This process also applies to meditating. I call this problem 'resistance'. When you become aware of it, drop your excuses and thoughts of 'I'll just do this or that first' take yourself by the scruff of the neck and go to your meditation place to meditate.

Resistance is a mind game. You may recall

how a small child will suddenly find something very interesting that must be done when mother says it is bedtime.

The thinking mind is the same, it resists being managed, imagining that it is not in control. This is the way I see it, why else would you not do something that is so enjoyable and good for you!

Everyone goes through phases of resistance and unless you recognise this and acknowledge it, you may give up meditating as not being for you.

3.4 Body sensations

Beginners are often affected by bodily sensations. For many people, the experience of observing one's breathing can be quite unsettling and at first you may even feel a bit panicky or feel tightness in the chest. I cannot give you a scientific explanation for this phenomenon. I feel it may be due to the mind not wishing to lose its hold on you. So just accept the experience until it passes, as it surely will do.

Another common sensation is awareness of the heart beat. For a little while the heart may feel like it is racing. No need to panic, just notice it, stay with it, smile at it and be gentle with yourself until it settles down. Interestingly our breathing rate and heart rate are varying all the time to meet the body's need to take in oxygen and let go of carbon dioxide. For the most part we are unaware of the changes. The heart and lungs can function without our conscious control. But the mind can also consciously increase the heart rate and breathing rate. When the mind imagines it is threatened, it can trigger a physical response very quickly.

This can sometimes happen when you first start to meditate, and those people with a tendency to panic attacks may equate these symptoms as an onset of panic. It appears that the thinking mind sees meditation as losing control (which of course it is), and so it creates diversions like bodily sensations to protect itself.

To overcome these sensations, be accepting of them. Be gentle with yourself and reassure yourself that everything is all right. Nothing bad will happen. Give it time to pass, and then start your meditation technique. Do not try to push the sensations out of your mind by scolding yourself or forcing ideas on yourself.

What you resist persists, so just be with the sensations and know that they will pass.

Occasionally I experience a hissing sound in my ears where I feel I am sinking.

When this happens I just say to myself 'There's the strange sensation again' and notice it passing.

3.5 Fidgets

Sometimes I can take what seems ages to settle down to watching my breathing.

I have an itch that needs rubbing, or my clothes are uncomfortable and need adjusting, or I see a speck of fluff on my sleeve or I feel shivers. How to overcome the fidgets? Give in to them for a few minutes then do some deep breathing and let go, watching any fidgets just pass away. Smile to yourself, 'There go the fidgets again!'

If this happens often, check that you are not hungry, or needing the toilet. Do a few stretching exercises first or change into more comfortable clothes.

Finally, make sure the room is not cold. I have had to meditate in some draughty, cold places in my time! Not good!

Sometimes fidgets arise during meditation. If you need to react, like rubbing an itch or blowing your nose, do so! It's no big deal, be gentle with yourself. Once the fidget has passed, return to watching the breathing, noticing the outbreath.

3.6 Feelings and emotions

There may be an occasion during your meditation when a sad memory arises, accompanied by tearfulness, or there may simply be strong emotion without a story.

In these situations, allow yourself to fully experience the emotion. Once you feel calmer return to noticing your breathing and waiting for the outbreath. Then you will be able to see the emotional release with compassion for yourself. As I have explained before the meditation process clears negativity that we have held onto, often unknowingly. In my experience, the release of emotions during meditation is healing and brings in positive energy.

3.7 Sleepiness

The process of meditation requires you to be alert and aware. But sometimes you may find you fall asleep. It doesn't matter, you are obviously tired so don't be hard on yourself. However, if it is happening frequently, then you need to look at why. For me the early evening about five o'clock is my low energy time.

Then I need something to eat and drink, and maybe a ten minute nap (if I'm lucky!). I know it is no use me trying to meditate at that time. It may help to notice when you have a low energy time and avoid going to meditate then.

If you have had a large meal, and/or alcohol this will make you sleepy. It is also advisable not to meditate lying down, or in bed as these postures are triggers for relaxation. If your meditation chair is too comfy, you may like to try sitting on a stool and check that the room is not too warm.

For some of us, closing our eyes is a trigger for sleep. To overcome this tendency in meditation, have the eyelids slightly open, gazing downwards with a soft focus. Allow your gaze to rest in one small area rather than letting your attention move around.

3.8 Expectation

This is another hindrance to meditation. When you first start practising meditation you may have one or two 'good' sessions and then when following sessions don't meet up with previous 'good' ones it is easy to lose heart. Even when you have been meditating for a number of years, expectation can creep up on you.

You may have slept badly, or be worried about the events happening in the day.

You may have had a stressful day and be planning a busy evening. Or as I have at times, you may become blasé about preparing to meditate and experience restlessness. Because we bring a variety of experiences to each session, each meditation is bound to be different from the previous one, so have no expectation of how the meditation should be. This means following the guidelines, trusting the process and letting it just be as it is.

Meditation is doing the business of clearing in its own gentle way — clearing out rubbish we have hung on to for years and bringing you to know what is at the foundation of your being — stillness.

3.9 Restlessness

There are times during a meditation when feelings of restlessness arise.

Occasionally I feel as if I don't want to meditate any longer even though I may have been sitting for only five minutes.

Negative thoughts arise, such as 'This is a waste of time' or 'Why am I doing this when I could be relaxing on the sofa with a book and a cuppa?'

Sometimes the restlessness is so strong that I just get up and walk about for a while and start over. But most times I can notice the restlessness until it passes, as it always does, and then start again, watching for the outbreath.

3.10 Upset and worry

We all experience episodes of strong turbulent thoughts and emotions, due to a recent upset like a break up with a close friend, or a loss of someone dear to us.

Or for example, we worry about what might happen to us when an unexpected health problem comes for ourselves or a loved one.

In extremely stressful times, it can be difficult to settle to meditate, even though this is a time when meditation is most helpful. Often my students will say that when they are upset about something they cannot bring themselves to meditate.

For situations like this, a different type of meditation can work well. This is called 'Loving kindness' meditation and it is track 5 on the CD.

I have written Section 4.2 on this meditation technique for a more in depth explanation.

3.11 Time

When you start meditating without the CD, you may wonder how you will know when to finish your session. Generally you will find that you automatically open your eyes after twenty minutes as if you have programmed yourself, and looking at your clock confirms this. Occasionally, you will look at the clock thinking that you have been sitting for twenty minutes when in fact you have only been there for five minutes or so. In such a situation, just start again by noticing your breathing as you do at the beginning of the meditation and carry on until you have completed twenty minutes in total.

It is simply that the concept of time is skewed in meditation.

3.12 It isn't working for me

If you follow the first or second track on the CD I can assure you that the process is working. Trust me on this! I do understand this thought and it is a mind game.

You may have the sensation that you only reach stillness for a very short time before thoughts arise again. But you cannot measure stillness during meditation.

Time stops still!

There is inhalation, then exhalation and then there is stillness until the next inhalation.

Thoughts come and go, and then there is stillness until the next thought arises.

When people first start to meditate, it can occasionally happen that the first few sessions feel busy and unsettling. But that soon passes. So if it is happening to you, stick with it and trust the process is working. Because it definitely is!

Occasionally there may be a meditation where you feel you are not 'centred' on your mind and body's activities. This is just a thought, like any other. You can be sure that if you follow CD track 1 or 2 the meditation is doing the business of clearing negativity. You need only be disturbed by the doorbell or telephone to realised how 'centred' you are.

❧ Part Four ❧

Other meditation techniques

4.1 Using a mantra

A mantra is a word or series of words that one repeats vocally or mentally. They are used for different purposes. The system of using mantras is based on Tibetan and Indian philosophies. And some teachers study the hundreds of different mantras to select the 'right' mantra for their individual followers.

When I first learned to meditate, I was given a mantra to use. The mantra was given to me verbally, not written down. It is not intended to have a meaning or translation as the sound creates an inner vibration within the body to assist in clearing negativity and promote healing. To meditate using a one word mantra, you repeat the word over and over, and as the mind becomes quiet, the mantra seems to disappear. When thoughts arise again, you start repeating the mantra again.

When the mind is very busy and you are unable to settle down to meditate, using a mantra can be quite helpful. I have deliberately not written the mantra down in the book. The reason for this is that when you see the word written down, the mind starts to explore, interpret and put meaning into the sound. For the purpose of meditation the sounds have no meaning.

I used the mantra meditation technique for a couple of years before changing to meditating on the outbreath, and it is one good way of starting meditating. The reason I changed from using a mantra to observing my breathing was through a chance reading of a beautiful translation of the Bhagavad Gita (an ancient Sanskrit text) in which there is a description of meditation on the breath. I decided to work on this, hence evolved my own 'bread and butter' technique.

For me, the value of observing the breathing is that I am also able to witness my thoughts, sensations, emotions for what they really are, and I am able to experience stillness effortlessly.

Other types of mantras are used in spiritual devotions and invocations. Many Tibetan and Indian mantras are based on the word 'OM' which translates as the First Word. There are thousands of different mantras and they are used in the same way as chants are in other cultures.

Some of the mantras also act on the body by resonating and vibrating to achieve an altered state of consciousness. Many are used by groups of meditators, such as 'Om mani padme Om', which is used as a chant for the benefit of all sentient beings. Although I am no expert on the vast subject of mantras, I have found their use very helpful, and energizing when used in a group situation.

4.2 Loving Kindness Meditation

In times of upset or anxiety it can be difficult to settle down to meditate on the outbreath.

This meditation is very helpful and easy to follow, and you will find that your heightened emotions and mental activity soon calm down when you use this technique. (Track 5 on the CD).

Remember to begin by observing your breathing for a few moments.

When you feel ready, start to repeat the following meditation to yourself over and over again for about fifteen minutes. You can say the words out loud to start with, then continue to say them internally.

> May I be happy
> May I be well
> May I be safe
> May I be at ease

At first repeat each statement one after the other without a break, then as the mind and emotions calm down, break for a couple of seconds between each statement, thus allowing you to experience peacefulness. Gradually increase the gap between each statement.

Like this: 'May I be happy................ May I be well........May I be safe.......... May I be at ease'

Thoughts and feelings during meditation are natural. Simply let go of the thought and return to saying the Loving Kindness.

After ten minutes or more, you may like to send loving kindness to someone you love. Visualize the person, and imagine them surrounded by love. Silently say, 'May you be happy' etc. Then finish by sending loving kindness to yourself again.

4.3 Thankfulness

This is a contemplation technique, not a meditation. But I wanted to share it with you because I find it very useful.

I am sure, like me, you often say you are thankful for something that arises without realizing you have said so. But when you notice what being thankful *feels* like, it brings positive energy to you. In my experience it is not possible to feel negative when you are thankful. You can turn a negative experience into a positive feeling with thankfulness. For example, I can say 'Even though the injections were very painful I am thankful that they made me well'

So we can turn negative experiences into positive ones. 'Even though my previous partner abused me, I am thankful that it showed me how I want my present relationship to be.'

There have been events in my past that I have found very painful, and they've kept coming back to 'haunt' me. You know what I mean; it is the same set of thoughts that flash into the mind from years back. One instance, when I was four years old, and at school, two big boys lifted me up and sat me in a puddle of water and they took me to the teacher and told her I had wee'd my pants. I was so upset that I had been treated this way.

Using thankfulness, I can say 'Even though this was a very painful memory for me, I am thankful that I know what it feels like to be victimized so that I will never victimize another. This is just a simple example to show you how you can deal with persistent negative thoughts from the past. I know it seems simplistic but it does work!

It seems we store negative experiences somewhere in our psyche and the memories crop up when we least expect them!

I have experienced this during meditation. I recall that during a meditation I had memories of being really hurt by a school friend forty five years ago. I had forgotten all about it and couldn't even remember her name. But the memory felt acutely painful even after all that time.

After that particular meditation, I thought about what had happened and how it must have stuck with me. I decided to deal with it like this. First of all, I was thankful that the meditation process had brought this to the surface and then I was able to release the painful experience by being thankful to the one who caused me pain. 'Even though you hurt me very much, I am thankful to you because I have learned to consider the feelings of others'.

It is worth remembering that the meditation process only brings past negative experiences into your awareness when you are ready to deal with them and let them go.

Another use of thankfulness is bringing positive situations to oneself in the future.

Be thankful for something you choose to have for yourself and watch it turn up.

Be thankful for the perfect car parking space! It's a sort of Knowing that it is going to happen and thanking its arrival in advance.

Yet another use of thankfulness is to look at something you have and take for granted. This is a helpful technique when you can't get to sleep or when you are stuck in traffic. Once you have tried this contemplation you will find you can use it in all sorts of situations! Here is an example to show you how it works.

Consider the banana in your breakfast bowl.

Now you can go into as much detail as you like!

'I am thankful that I have this banana to eat. I am thankful that the shop is there for me to buy the banana.

I am thankful to the person who delivered it to the store. I am thankful to the person who shipped it from Jamaica. I am thankful to the people who tended the crop. I am thankful to the banana tree that produced the fruit in my bowl. I am thankful for the earth that produced the plant and the rain that watered the plant so that I can enjoy my banana'.

When you have gone through this entire process, you can't help but laugh and appreciate the very simplest things in life, and feel at ease within.

❧ Finally ❧

If this CD and book have helped you to start meditating, then I have achieved what I set out to do.

If you can introduce someone else to meditation, then you too are giving them a skill for living and the gift of peace within.

Meditation is simple.

Just turn up!

❦ Acknowledgements ❦

Thank you my dear family and friends for your encouragement and support.

Thank you John and Gwyneth at Fast Forward recording studios for your patience in producing my CD.

Thank you Trafford for making my dream book a reality.

About the Author

Georgina Smith lives near Sherwood Forest in Nottinghamshire with her husband Mike and their two dogs, Molly and Mitzi. She is mother to Alistair and Rebecca and nanna to Elena, Grace and Ralph.

Georgina's career was as a registered nurse and she also qualified as a teacher. Her interest in nursing led to a parallel interest in healing, and she is a Reiki Master Teacher and a healer member of the NFSH. Since she retired she works as a volunteer for a group supporting families of drug and alcohol users, and runs a meditation group for the local community. Georgina also has individual clients for healing and meditation.

Her other interests are learning to play the piano, playing bridge, cooking, walking, racehorses, and enjoying time with family and friends.

Central to her daily life is meditation which has been pivotal to her own personal development. She learned meditation twenty years ago and since then has explored its many facets. The CD and book are the culmination of all her knowledge and personal experience of many years of practising meditation whilst leading a busy life at work and at home.

You may contact Georgina at
www..just-turn-up.co.uk

Notes

Notes